CONTENTS

Chapter 1

Understanding Depression and Suicidal Thoughts

Troy was fifteen when he began feeling hopeless. His family was having money problems, he was being bullied at school, and he started to think that there was no way out of his problems. He couldn't imagine continuing to hide his sexuality from his neighbors in his small town. Troy didn't believe anyone would accept him for who he was. Feeling like his pain would never end, Troy attempted suicide.

Opposite: Anyone can suffer from feelings of hopelessness that lead to suicidal thoughts. Pay attention to what you're thinking and feeling, and ask for help if you need it.

Troy's suicide attempt was more than twenty years ago. Today, he has a family of his own, and he leads a life of joy and purpose. Troy's recovery was a long road. "There are still days that suicide pops into my head," he says. "But … I've been given tools and I have support, and I know that there are solutions to whatever it is that is going on."

Troy's story is not uncommon. Adults who attempted suicide in their teens often say that many of the problems they faced then are no longer relevant to their lives. Others continue to struggle with suicidal thoughts but have the coping skills they need to thrive anyway.

More and more parents, teachers, friends, and classmates are coming to terms with the seriousness of depression and suicidal thoughts. Communities are finding new ways to reach out to suicidal teens. This work is critical. You are in a position to help yourself and others and to make a difference in the epidemic of teen suicide.

If you or someone you love is in danger of harming themselves right now, please call 911. The phone number for the National Suicide Prevention Lifeline (United States) is 1-800-273-8255. If you are in Canada, you can call the Canada Suicide Prevention Service: 1-833-456-4566.

A GROWING PROBLEM

As of 2016, suicide is the second-leading cause of death for Americans under the age of eighteen. The Centers for Disease Control (CDC) reports that the total number of teen suicides increased 70 percent from 2006 to 2016. Experts believe that more than 15 percent of all high school students have seriously considered suicide by the time they graduate.

These numbers mean that it is likely that some of your friends, the people sitting next to you in class, and even your siblings might be grappling with suicidal thoughts. For a number of teens, the transition into adulthood can be difficult. Adolescents can be a particularly vulnerable group that can encounter pressure from their family and peer group. Many often encounter some of the following pressures and problems:

- Family breakdown

- Sexuality (teenage pregnancy, sexually transmitted diseases, sexual identity issues)

- Body image (anorexia nervosa, bulimia, obesity, acne)

- Moral and spiritual (conflict with parental values, rebellion, susceptibility to religious groups and cults)

- School achievement

- Peer pressure

- Social challenges

Teens may experience one of these problems or several at once. For teens who suffer from mental health conditions like depression or substance abuse problems, these stressors might feel like too much to bear.

TEENS AND DEPRESSION

Depression is a medical condition on the rise in teens. Those aged fifteen to twenty-four suffer the highest rate of depression and suicidal thoughts, but only 30 percent of depressed teens get help.

Chances are someone sitting next to you in one of your classes is struggling. Reaching out could save a life.

Using the Right Words

The words you use when talking about suicide can help others feel safe sharing their experiences. Avoid saying someone "committed" suicide.

Because suicide is such a sensitive topic, it's important to use the correct terms when discussing it. Mental health professionals advise against saying that someone "committed suicide," or that someone made a "successful" or "unsuccessful" suicide attempt. Instead, experts recommend using the term "died by suicide," saying that someone "ended their life," or that he or she made a "nonfatal" or "fatal" suicide attempt. There are good reasons for these word choices.

"Died by suicide" does not make it sound like someone committed a crime or a sin. Calling suicide attempts "fatal" or "nonfatal" just communicates facts without any judgment. On the other hand, labeling suicide attempts as "successful" or "unsuccessful" can encourage people who have made nonfatal suicide attempts to make further suicide attempts. Suicide-attempt survivors who seek treatment have reported feeling like failures after hearing people call their attempts "unsuccessful."

Psychologists and psychiatrists encourage everyone to choose their words carefully after someone dies by suicide. It's important to make sure that friends and family left behind feel like they can talk openly about their loved one. It's also critical to remember that every time you talk about suicide, someone listening might be struggling with suicidal thoughts. The way that you talk about suicide could be the difference between them asking for help or hiding their pain.

There is a direct link between depressive illnesses and suicide. It is important to note that teens who are feeling depressed do not necessarily feel suicidal. It is also very important to know that not all suicidal teens are depressed.

Depression's Warning Signs

It is not unusual to feel sad, blue, or even depressed from time to time. Sadness is a normal reaction to loss or grieving. On the other hand, sometimes feeling down becomes so intense that it interferes with day-to-day living. People can get depressed for many reasons: genetic factors, loss of a personal relationship, illness, grief, feeling alone, poor self-esteem, feeling like a failure in life, abusing alcohol and drugs, or a number of intense life disappointments.

Depression is an internal state. The image that people who are depressed show to the rest of the world may not reveal the true desperation they are, in fact, experiencing internally. Some exhibit a few, and some experience many, of the following signs of depression:

- Losing interest in hobbies, school, and friends

- Experiencing a lot of aches and pains

- Feeling blue, Rebellious, and angry

- Sleeping too much or too little

- Letting hygiene go

Depression gets in the way of day-to-day life. Look out for symptoms in yourself and others.

- Low energy

- Crying spells

- Trouble with day-to-day concentration or memory

- Persistent sad, anxious, or empty mood

- Feelings of hopelessness and pessimism

- Feelings of guilt, worthlessness, and helplessness

- Fatigue

- Difficulty making decisions

- Weight loss or gain

- Restlessness and irritability

- Persistent symptoms such as headaches, digestive disorders, and chronic pain

- Thoughts of death and suicide

- Suicide attempts

Many of these characteristics are common in teenagers, but the time to be concerned is when roughly five or more are prevalent or if a teen has suicidal thoughts or makes an attempt on their own life.

Kinds of Depression

Depression doesn't come in just one form. There are many different types of depression. In seasonal affective disorder (SAD), people who have difficulties adjusting to less sunlight during the winter months feel depressed and blue. Bipolar disorder is a mental disorder that can be seen as a wide variance of mood. People with bipolar disorder are sometimes depressed and sometimes experience mania, which is when a person is hyperactive, highly elated, or irritable. Someone who is bipolar has mood swings between these two states.

Clinical depression means that the depression is severe enough to require treatment. A person who is clinically depressed feels sad most of the day, nearly every day, for at least two weeks. Often the person cannot sleep or sleeps too much. Clinically

Bullying can take place in person, online, or through text messages. There is a link between bullying and depression, so it's important to report bullying immediately.

depressed people lose interest in activities that they once enjoyed, lose their sense of value for themselves, and feel worthless and helpless. Because they have a severe loss or increase in appetite, a weight change may start to become noticeable. For adolescents, depression may appear like irritability. Self-destructive behavior may be common when dealing with depressive states. This behavior may take more indirect forms such as acting out and self-destructive behaviors such as cutting (using a knife on the skin) or alcohol and drug abuse.

Attempting suicide is a more direct and highly lethal form of self-harm. Clinically depressed adolescents are significantly more likely to attempt suicide than their nondepressed peers. In treating clinical depression, many professionals work with antidepressant medications. Depression and its warning signs should be taken very seriously. The sooner depression can be identified and treated, the better.

Bullying and Depression

Researchers have found a relationship between bullying and clinical depression in teens.

Bullying incidents have been reported during all levels in school from primary grades to high schools. Bullying incidents have also been reported at the

Text Messages, Cyberbullying, and the Death of Conrad Roy

Michelle Carter appears in court during her trial in 2017.

In 2014, eighteen-year-old Conrad Roy III ended his life. He left behind a loving family and his seventeen-year-old girlfriend, Michelle Carter. Roy's suicide would end up making international news, and Carter would find herself in prison for it.

After a 2017 trial, a Massachusetts judge found that Carter's text messages to Roy convinced Roy to take his own life. In her text messages, Carter repeated myths and lies about suicide. She told Roy that dying by suicide was the way to end his pain. After Roy's death, Carter told a friend that she "could've easily stopped him or called the police but I didn't." Carter was convicted on involuntary manslaughter and sentenced to two and a half years in prison.

Carter's prison sentence shows cyberbullying can come from surprising places, including friends, girlfriends, or boyfriends. The Carter case is an extreme reminder that everyone is responsible for what they say online and via text message. Words carry a lot of weight— and digital words have real-life consequences.

college level and even in the workforce. Many school boards have curricula that address the problem of bullying. Some have help lines to assist victims of bullying.

Bullying can take place in person or online. While most interactions online are positive, there are those who use the internet to antagonize and intimidate people. Cyberbullying is a way to harass, humiliate, or threaten others using the internet or cell phones.

Report bullying to a trusted adult, like a coach, parent, teacher, or guidance counselor.

There are many cases where cyberbullying has been one of the main causes for young people to end their lives. In fact, experts say that victims of cyberbullying are twice as likely to hurt themselves.

If you have ever been bullied, you cannot help but feel disempowered. Many students who kill themselves were bullied by others and could not break the painful cycle. They saw suicide as a way out from the day-to-day torment. It's important to remember that there are solutions to bullying.

First, be aware of what you are posting on websites. If you have a blog, be very careful what it contains. Go to an adult if you read anything online or have a circumstance that you feel uncomfortable handling yourself or if you are feeling threatened in any way. In general, always guard your private contact information. Do not give people you do not know any information about yourself, like your cell phone number, name, address, school, or email address.

If you are being bullied on the internet, you need to save the evidence. Don't keep looking at it, as this may create more stress. You should store it in a place where you can access it later. Next, send an assertive message telling the bully to stop harassing you, and block or filter all messages from the bully.

If you've done those things, and the bully is still harassing you, change your email address, block the bully on social media accounts, and tell your school counselor or a teacher. If the cyberbully is a peer, have your parent contact his or her parents or guardians to let them know what is going on. If you continue to be bullied, have your parent contact a lawyer to send a letter demanding the cyberbullying stop. Contact the police if the cyberbullying involves threats of violence, coercion, obscene messages, harassment or stalking, hate or bias messages, or if he or she is creating or sending sexually explicit pictures.

BUSTING MYTHS ABOUT TEEN SUICIDE

Contrary to popular belief that suicides occur around holidays, such as Thanksgiving, Christmas, and

New Year's, research indicates that suicide is most prevalent in the spring. People usually die by suicide during the daytime. Less than half of people who die by suicide leave a note. Many times, suicide attempts are actually cries for help that need to be taken seriously. The act is a way of communicating the intense turmoil the person is feeling. Many teens do not actually want to end their lives; they want an end to the pain they are feeling.

There is a lot of misinformation about suicide floating around. This misinformation can stand between people and the help they need. Below are some common myths about suicide attempts and suicidal thoughts. Understanding the truth about suicide and suicidal thoughts is the first step toward beating the stigma that surrounds it.

Myth: Friends Should Not Tell on a Friend Who Is Talking About Suicide

Fact: It is difficult to betray a friend's trust, and you may worry he or she is going to be angry with you, but by telling a responsible adult, you may in fact be saving your friend's life. This is one secret you should not keep.

Myth: Once a Teen Is Suicidal, He or She Is Suicidal for His or Her Entire Life

Fact: Many times people can feel suicidal for a limited time, and with the proper interventions and preventive measures, their behavior can be controlled. It is important to note that being suicidal is not necessarily a life sentence.

Myth: People Who Talk About Suicide Will Not Attempt It

Fact: People who talk about suicide do quite often make attempts, including fatal attempts. If a teenager mentions that he or she is thinking of suicide, do not brush it off or laugh it off; take the threat very seriously. Eighty percent of people give many clues to the fact that they are going to attempt to take their own lives. This means that if you know ten people who constantly talk about suicide, eight of those ten may try it, so take it seriously.

Myth: Suicide Affects Only One Member of a Family

Fact: Some families do have a history of suicide. Suicidal behavior is not necessarily predetermined genetically, but there is a major concern that once a suicide exists in a family, other members may be at high risk. What is hereditary is a predisposition for depression, which can lead to suicidal thoughts. Nowadays, with medication and counseling, high-risk family members can be helped. Just because one member of a family has died by suicide does not mean another member of the family is doomed to take their own life.

Myth: People Who Survive a Suicide Attempt Never Try Again

Fact: Half of all teens who have made one suicide attempt will make another, sometimes more than one a year until they take their own life. In fact, three months to a year after the first attempt, repeat attempts have been noted to occur, even when it looks like the person may be improving. That is the strange thing—just when you think the person looks happier, he or she may try and take his or her own life again. The issues and the problems that led to the suicide attempt need to be altered or changed, otherwise the person may likely try again. The majority of suicide attempts are expressions of extreme distress and not just harmless bids for attention. Those teens who have had a suicide attempt should be carefully monitored.

Myth: Suicide Is Painless

Fact: Many suicide methods are in fact painful. The media sometimes portrays suicide attempts romantically, but the reality is they can be very harsh.

Myth: People from Good Families Never Die by Suicide

Fact: Suicide can claim people from all walks of life, religion, socioeconomic stature, and age. For example, a teenager may feel that he or she is in a perfect family but feels he or she can never be good enough. It's critical to not let shame about yourself or your family stand in the way of getting help.

Chapter 2

Teens at Risk

Throughout middle school and high school, Emily's friends gossiped about her, excluded her, and constantly told her she wasn't like them. Their bullying got so bad that Emily began thinking about ending her life. Luckily, Emily sought treatment for depression and found a refuge online, where she made friends who understood what she was going through.

Emily was at high risk for experiencing suicidal thoughts. Social isolation and bullying are two

Opposite: Julia Hansen (*center*) started the Yellow Tulip Project after two of her closest friends died by suicide. The Yellow Tulip Project works to "smash the stigma surrounding mental illness."

common risk factors for teen suicide. Understanding risk factors and at-risk groups can help you understand yourself better and help you identify peers who need help.

RISK FACTORS

Many teens go through their lives dealing with their responsibilities in healthy ways. There are those, however, who will find themselves in risky situations and have difficulties coping with them. Risk factors are circumstances that may predispose a person to consider or attempt suicide. (Remember that not all risk factors lead to suicide.)

Some of the main risk factors include:

- Alcohol and drug abuse

- Gambling

- School and/or personal crisis

- Setting high self-standards

- Legal problems

- Social isolation

- Trouble at home

- Bullying

- Unplanned pregnancy

- Previous suicide attempt

- Depression

- Media influence and cluster suicides (copycat suicides)

- New situations like beginning college

- Chemical imbalances

- Early traumas

- Sexual identity issues

Alcohol and Drug Abuse

Drugs and alcohol are used by many teens to attempt to reduce the pain they are feeling from stress and feelings of helplessness or hopelessness. Teens can start feeling signs of depression as early as age twelve or thirteen. If they do not seek professional help, depressed teens may seek out other methods to relieve themselves of their symptoms. They may turn to drugs and alcohol to help them deal with their pain. Teens who engage in high-risk behaviors involving sex and alcohol and drugs have significantly higher odds of suicidal thoughts and suicide attempts.

When a person first starts to drink alcohol, it can elevate their mood, but it is in fact a depressant drug. Having two to three glasses of alcohol can impair one's vision, speech, coordination, and sense of balance, and can cause loss of self-control. If a teen already suffers from depression, alcohol can increase his or her feelings. If a teen is feeling suicidal, these feelings may become enhanced after drinking alcohol. The relationship between alcoholism and suicide appears to be stronger among males than females.

Research shows that among young people who took their own lives, the drugs most commonly abused after alcohol were marijuana, cocaine, amphetamines, and combinations of the three. Also, young people who have not been known to have suicidal feelings before may become vulnerable to depression and suicidal emotions under the influence of drugs and alcohol, particularly after prolonged use.

Studies of middle schoolers and high schoolers show that teens who abstain from drugs and alcohol have the lowest levels of depression, suicidal thoughts, and suicide attempts. Teens who report heavy use of illegal drugs like marijuana had the highest level. Research also shows that girls compared to boys were less likely to pursue high-risk behaviors, but when they did, they were more vulnerable to depression, suicidal thoughts, and suicide attempts.

High-risk behaviors can contribute to suicidal behavior in many teenagers. Young people who are depressed could also be more drawn to drugs as a form of self-medication and escape. A 2012 study found that about one-fourth of all suicide victims in the United States had consumed alcohol prior to taking their lives. Experts believe that teen suicide victims might be even more likely to be intoxicated at time of death.

Kevin Breel's Story

As a teen, Kevin Breel had a life that looked perfect from the outside. He was the captain of the basketball team, he earned great grades, and he had a lot to look forward to. Breel also had a secret. He was grappling with depression, and he was thinking about taking his own life. In fact, Breel says that he considered suicide every day of his life.

Today, Breel has made it his mission to tackle the stigma surrounding depression. In a viral TED Talk, Breel told the world his secret. Being open and honest changed his life for the better. He has a brand-new perspective about what life with depression can look like, and he says that being open about his problems is the key. In Breel's words:

Unfortunately, we live in a world where if you break your arm, everyone runs over to sign your cast, but if you tell people you're depressed, everyone runs the other way. That's the stigma. We are so, so, so accepting of any body part breaking down other than our brains. And that's ignorance. That's pure ignorance, and that ignorance has created a world that doesn't understand depression, that doesn't understand mental health.

Through his activism and honesty, Breel works toward making others feel less alone. "Depression is okay," he says. "If you're going through it, know that you're okay. And know that you're sick, you're not weak, and it's an issue, not an identity."

Gambling

Gamblers have the highest suicide rate of any addicted group. Some teens see gambling as a way to make easy money. What they cannot envision is the cycle of losing and going into debt. Many teens who constantly gamble on the internet, sometimes winning and many times losing, are isolated. They start craving the thrill of the win and of course get despondent, or let down, at the loss. Some teens might lose large sums of money, causing them to feel overwhelmed, hopeless, and ashamed. The simplest way to avoid a gambling addiction is to never start. However, there are resources for teens who find themselves developing a gambling problem. If you or a peer have a gambling addiction, reach out to a trusted adult, like a school counselor. They can help you find a therapist, treatment program, or support group.

Cluster Suicides

When a celebrity dies by suicide, statistics show a spike in the number of suicides after the news story breaks. This phenomenon is known as a cluster, or copycat, suicide. Cluster suicides can also occur in communities, families, and schools. Researchers say that the "suicidal contagion" behind cluster suicides affects teens the most. Of course, suicide is not actually contagious. Just because there have been high-profile suicides or suicides that have affected you personally does not mean that more people around you are going to die by suicide. That said, knowing that cluster suicides can occur helps you to be on the lookout for peers who might be at a higher risk.

School and Personal Problems

School is often stressful for teens. There is the stress of passing tests, completing day-to-day homework, getting into a college or university, being popular, and basically fitting in. There are also the physical, sexual, and emotional changes that occur through adolescence. This is a time of rapid change. It is also a time for moods to be somewhat erratic. Most of this is quite normal. It is when a teen is feeling out of control and in crisis that the need for help must be addressed.

Some school problems can be attributed to students having difficulties with academics, perhaps

The stress of tests, homework, and grades can take a toll on students.

because of learning disabilities. At times, school problems can be a warning sign of deeper issues. They may be a sign that a teen is feeling depressed.

Adolescence is also the time when young men and women start getting romantically involved. With relationships come breakups. Teens of both genders have attempted suicide because they could not cope with their romantic breakups, though historically this has been more prevalent among females. Young women are also more prone to anorexia nervosa, an eating disorder in which people restrict their food intake. In some cases, anorexia leads to death, a slow suicide.

Many teens feel there is an "in crowd" and that they are not part of it. If a teen has trouble making friends, this can be cause for concern. It's fairly easy to look around and identify peers who are loners. Many times, teens do not empathize or put themselves in the other person's shoes. Social isolation can be extremely painful. Reaching out to others can literally save lives.

Teens' lives are busy and complicated. Juggling family, school, friendships, and relationships can be difficult.

On the other hand, some students who take their own lives seem to have it all. Setting high standards and not achieving them, as well as family pressures of setting overly high expectations to excel, can also be problems. These are anxious, insecure teens who have a desperate desire to be liked, to fit in, and to do well. Their expectations are so high that they demand too much of themselves and are condemned to constant disappointment.

Being a teenager is not an easy experience. There are times when you are feeling up and times when you are feeling down. It is when the down times and the negative feelings start to take over that the need to get help and support is crucial.

HIGH-RISK GROUPS

Suicidal thoughts can affect anyone. Yet there are a number of high-risk groups that are vulnerable and show more incidence of depression and suicidal thoughts than other groups. Some of these groups are Native American teens; Indigenous Canadian teens; African American teens; Hispanic teens; and gay, bisexual, or transgender teens.

In 2015, 5,486 American youths died by suicide. Of those young people, 3,672 were white, 807 were Hispanic, 574 were African American, 265 were Asian, and 150 were Native American. These totals don't tell the full story, though. Many of these numbers indicate large increases in suicide cases for a particular ethnic group over time. Furthermore, total numbers fail to show the percentage of youths of a given ethnicity who attempt suicide or take their own life. Studies often discuss the number of deaths or attempts per one hundred thousand people of a given population. This percentage is also known as the suicide rate.

Native Americans

Native Americans have the second-highest suicide rate of any ethnicity, after white people. According to the Suicide Prevention Resource Center, "Among American Indians and Alaska Natives, suicide rates peak during adolescence and young adulthood, then decline." The center notes that this is "a very different pattern than the overall age pattern [for suicide] in the United States." Typically, the risk for suicide peaks at middle age.

Depression and suicide are huge problems among Native teens. They have to live in a world where racism is on the rise. When teens feel there is nowhere to go, some turn to alcohol abuse and drugs to deal with their depression. In a 2018 survey, one in four Native American middle schoolers surveyed said they had been intoxicated. Drug and alcohol abuse also affect the Indigenous population in Canada. In 2017, researchers found that among Indigenous youth who were drug users when they died, the third-leading cause of death was suicide.

Native Americans and Indigenous Canadians have specific risk factors, such as:

- Poverty

- Rapid culture change and/or cultural discontinuity (their life as they once knew it is rapidly disappearing)

- Forced assimilation (being absorbed by larger society without a choice.)

- Forced Relocation (being forced off their Native lands)

- School experiences that exposed them to violence and abuse at a young age

- Copycat suicidal behaviors due to the close ties and identification among youth in small communities

There is a lot of hope, though. Culturally sensitive support groups, educational programs, and treatment facilities are important means of helping Native teens help themselves and their communities. In 2008, one such program was established by the Northwest Arctic Borough School District in Alaska. In the Youth Leaders Program, peer mentors help their classmates work through suicidal thoughts. More than ten years later, the program continues to save lives.

BLACK AND HISPANIC TEENS

Though the risk of suicide among young people is still highest with white males, suicide rates have increased for black and Hispanic teens. Additionally, the suicide rate for African Americans ages five through twelve is about double the rate of their white peers.

The CDC's 2015 Youth Risk Behavior Survey shows that Hispanic teens have the highest rate of suicide attempts. Hispanic females in particular report high rates of attempts. About 15 percent of

Hispanic females surveyed in 2015 said they had made a suicide attempt in the past year. These numbers are staggering compared to the 6.8 percent of white teens who attempted to take their own lives within the twelve months prior to the survey.

Black and Hispanic teens from lower socioeconomic backgrounds report that they had suicidal thoughts and said they had few adults in their lives with whom they could discuss their personal problems. Those who attempted suicide were more than twice as likely to report that they had no one to count on compared to a nonsuicidal group.

NATIONAL MINORITY
MENTAL HEALTH
AWARENESS MONTH
JULY 2018

OMH™ U.S. Department of
Health and Human Services
Office of Minority Health

National Minority Mental Health Awareness Month is held every July to promote awareness and end stigma.

Increasingly, schools and communities are speaking up about the stigma that keeps people from seeking help. In 2008, the US House of Representatives announced that July would be National Minority Mental Health Awareness Month. The goal is to "improve access to mental health treatment and services and promote public awareness of mental illness." With greater awareness and programs aimed at ending stigma, it is possible to reduce the risk of suicide for black and Hispanic teens.

Trevor Project staff and volunteers march in the Capital Pride Parade in Washington, DC.

Sexuality, Gender Identity, and Suicidal Thoughts

Gay, lesbian, and bisexual youth are three times more likely to attempt suicide than their heterosexual peers. Experts believe that each instance of bullying raises the chances that a gay, lesbian, or bisexual teen will hurt themselves by 2.5 times. And a 2016 study found that 30 percent of transgender youth had attempted suicide at least one time.

In 1998, Peggy Rajski, Randy Stone, and James Lecesne founded the Trevor Project, a foundation that aims to save the lives of LGBTQ youth through suicide prevention programs and resources. Through the TrevorLifeline (1-866-488-7386), TrevorChat (https://www.thetrevorproject.org/get-help-now), and TrevorText (text START to 678678), the Trevor Project provides crisis support to LGBTQ young people ages thirteen to twenty-four. Each year, the TrevorLifeline fields more than forty-five thousand calls. The Trevor Project is a powerful reminder that LGBTQ youth are not alone.

Celebrities' Stories

Dwayne "The Rock" Johnson has talked openly about experiencing depression.

Mental health issues can affect anyone. Fame, fortune, and opportunity don't prevent or lessen the chances that someone will face depression or suicidal thoughts. Many celebrities have opened up about their experiences with mental health conditions. Their stories demonstrate that popularity and success can't make someone immune from pain.

Stars like Cara Delevingne, Dwayne "The Rock" Johnson, Kendrick Lamar, and Lili Reinhart have spoken out about their depression. Drew Barrymore and Halle Berry have given interviews about suicide attempts. Many celebrities who speak up say that they do so to encourage fans to seek help when they need it.

Some celebrities have used their battles with depression as inspiration for songs, books, and charitable work. Lady Gaga started the Born This Way Foundation to help teens through depression and other common mental health issues. Rapper Logic's song "1-800-273-8255" is titled for the National Suicide Prevention Lifeline. Author J. K. Rowling says that the Dementors in the Harry Potter books were based on her experiences with depression. Rowling has given many interviews about her depression. She has even encouraged fans, tweeting, "The world is full of wonderful things you haven't seen yet. Don't ever give up on the chance of seeing them."

Chapter 3

Working Through Suicidal Thoughts

Every teen who has suicidal thoughts has a different experience. Some teens' suicidal thoughts come and go quickly, which is known as "passive suicidal ideation." Other teens experience constant thoughts of suicide. Their suicidal thoughts include detailed fantasies and involve making plans to end their lives. Experts call this "active suicidal ideation."

Opposite: With help, you can work through suicidal thoughts and move forward.

Many teens fall somewhere in between these two extremes. No matter where a teen falls on this spectrum, it's important for them to get help. When a friend is actively making plans to end their life, it is critical that you step in and tell an adult. If you are troubled by thoughts of suicide, speak up. Asking for help is an act of bravery that will change your life for the better.

KNOW THE WARNING SIGNS

Young people who have attempted suicide exhibit classic warning signs. When people talk about suicide, listen. When a teen starts making comments like he or she soon will not be hurting anymore, people will be sorry when he or she is gone, and everyone would be better off without him or her, these should make you concerned. Some other worrying signs are when your friend starts asking questions about dying, such as whether you think dying hurts. Your friend may indicate that he or she wants the sadness and depression to go away and

Sleeping a lot can be a sign of depression.

may want to do something about it. These are cries for help, and they must be heeded.

Some other signs that need immediate response include constantly talking about his or her own death, asking about different ways to kill oneself (learning the amount of a lethal dose of medication, how to get a gun, etc.), and actually saying he or she wants to take their own life.

Your friend may be preoccupied with books and music that have the common theme of suicide or be busy planning his or her own funeral. Obvious signs are when the person starts putting their affairs in order, making his or her final wishes known to friends and family, and giving away personal belongings.

Sometimes people may be influenced by someone close to them who has recently died by suicide. The grief over the loved one may be so overwhelming that they see suicide as the only answer. If you see the signs of depression after an event like this, the person should be persuaded to seek help.

It is always a concern when people appear to be withdrawn, with little interest about things and events around them. There is a reason to worry when someone's physical well-being starts to impact their day-to-day living, such as disruptive sleeping patterns (either too much or too little sleep), abnormal eating habits, and poor grooming, such as skipping showers or not brushing their hair. Persistent boredom and difficulty concentrating, especially at school, should also be alarms. Frequent physical complaints like stomachaches, headaches, and fatigue, as well as a sudden change in their grades, not completing homework, and losing interest in extracurricular activities may also be signs of depression that should be checked out.

Another serious sign is reckless behavior, like driving fast or taking drugs and not caring if he or she lives or dies. One of the most serious signs of impending suicide is when a person has been depressed for a long time or has already had a suicide attempt, and suddenly he or she cheers up. This could be a sign that he or she has made a decision to try to die.

HELPING SOMEONE IN NEED

When someone is thinking of suicide, try to encourage him or her to talk to a person who is trusted, such as a parent, a guardian, or a teacher. Maybe he or she needs to talk to a guidance counselor, social worker, or someone in the mental health profession. If it would be more comforting, encourage your friend to talk to a spiritual adviser or a member of his or her clergy.

It is important to be a good friend and listen. Try to explore the problem: What has been going on in the past couple of months? What has led up to the current situation? Always take your friend seriously, and do not make jokes about his or her feelings. Be interested in his or her emotions and actions. Remember to remain calm, be nonjudgmental, and offer appropriate options. If you think your friend is at risk, remove anything from his or her vicinity that could cause harm. Be there to offer any help or assistance. If it becomes over your head and the situation is turning into a crisis, tell a trusted adult. Remember, do not be sworn to secrecy. Seek help.

What you shouldn't do is debate whether suicide is right or wrong. Do not lecture on the value of life, and never dare the person to do it. **Don't** say:

- Don't worry, things will get better in time.

- It's not as bad as you think.

- You shouldn't feel that way.

- Other people have it much worse.

Finally, do not leave a suicidal person alone. Call a responsible member of the family, a crisis hotline, or if necessary, 911.

If you are with someone who is in crisis, call a suicide helpline. If your friend is in immediate danger, call 911.

GETTING HELP FOR YOURSELF

If someone were to ask you right now, at this present moment, if you were having thoughts of suicide, what would your answer be? If the answer is "maybe" or "yes," then this is a really difficult time for you. There is no reason to go through this time alone. If talking to your parents is not possible, try confiding in a trusted friend or an adult who knows you. "I think that some of my teachers in high school are the reason I'm here today," says nineteen-year-old Helene.

You may be starting to feel out of control and start experiencing sadness and signs of depression. You may feel that your life is a mess, lost and confused, that you have no effect on the outcome of your life, that your feelings are a blur, or you may be starting to have suicidal thoughts. When you are feeling suicidal, many times the emotional pain is great, and you can feel isolated in your pain. A lack of adequate coping techniques can contribute to this sense of helplessness and hopelessness.

Identifying Unhealthy
Coping Mechanisms

It is important for you to understand that you cannot eliminate stress entirely from your life, but you can learn how to manage it and reduce some of the distress it causes. You may not be able to control things, but you can control your reactions to those things. More positive ways to handle stress are through activities such as talking to someone who cares, exercising, listening to or playing music, and spending time with friends. When stressed, do you find yourself:

- Withdrawing into yourself?

- Resorting to self-abuse? (cutting, scratching until bleeding occurs, pulling out hair, bruising yourself, etc.)

- Resorting to self-destructive behaviors? (i.e., driving too fast)

- Using alcohol?

- Using drugs?

- Engaging in excessive risk-taking?

- Directing anger to either a specific object or a person?

If you are handling stress in a number of these ways, you need to consider getting outside support to learn how to take better care of your emotional well-being. If you are feeling depressed and suicidal, it is very important to talk to someone about what you are feeling. Finding someone to help is an act of wisdom and great courage.

People to Turn To

There are many teens who feel they would be rejected if people found out about their suicidal thoughts. Suicidal teens often hide their true feelings. Many times, the teen feels that he or she has nowhere to go. The pain is unbearable, and the teen sees suicide as their only choice. Here are some places where you can go for help before you take any further negative actions:

- Start at home with a parent or guardian or friend's parent.

You can always turn to a parent or trusted teacher if you need help.

- If that is not working, speak to a guidance counselor, an empathetic teacher, or a coach.

If you have a teacher whom you highly respect, tell him or her about your suicidal thoughts, even though it may be difficult. Take the risk. In most cases asking for help does get you the help you need.

- Make an appointment to see the school social worker, counselor, or psychologist as they are trained in suicide interventions.

- Teen volunteers or peer counselors working at crisis centers ask questions of other teens using their own experiences and at a teenage level. By talking with them, it could possibly lead you to get counseling.

- Call a crisis hotline. All conversations are confidential. These lines are manned by specially trained people to give you immediate support and can be helpful for you when you are in crisis. The people who work at the hotlines are trained to listen to you. They have discussions with you and learn about your problems and feelings of isolation. You can call back at any time if you feel suicidal or just need a helpful voice on the other end. They have had success in doing these immediate crisis interventions.

You may feel relief that you have started to share your inner thoughts, feelings, and pain with someone who empathizes and will listen to your emotional struggles. If you don't, don't give up. If the first person you approach does not provide the support you feel you need, find someone else. Find someone who is comfortable talking about suicide and working with you to prevent the risk of these thoughts leading to suicidal actions. Keep in mind:

- The person you approach may need to refer you on to somewhere else. He or she may be honest with you and feel you need more support than what he or she can provide. He or she may see that you need someone who can prescribe medications to help you with your depression.

- The person will want to keep you safe. You may need to go to the hospital if you are at high risk in order to get the support you need.

- It's essential that you are honest with the person you are talking to. Lies will just lead to more lies, and you will end up being caught up in them.

Suicide Hotlines

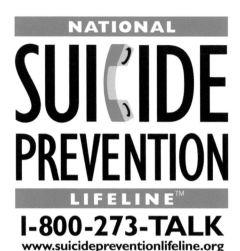

The National Suicide Prevention Lifeline has been helping people since 2004.

No matter the time of day or night, there are always trained professionals just a phone call away. If you need help, don't hesitate to call one of the following suicide hotlines. However, if you are in critical danger of hurting yourself or are with someone who is going to harm themselves, call 911.

National Suicide Prevention Lifeline
(United States)
1-800-273-8255

National Suicide Prevention Lifeline
en Español (United States)
1-888-628-9454

National Suicide Prevention Lifeline for
Individuals with Hearing Impairments
(United States)
1-800-799-4889

Canada Suicide Prevention
Service (Canada)
1-833-456-4566
1.866.277.3553 (for Quebec
residents)

The Crisis Text Line
Send a text message that says
"HOME" to 741741 (the United
States) or 686868 (Canada).

UNDERSTANDING COUNSELING

The most common method of dealing with suicidal behavior is doing some kind of talk therapy along with medication to help you through the depression. Counseling is a way to ask for help and talk about your problems with a trained therapist. It is objective, and the person cares what happens to you. It is a support to help you learn about yourself and how to cope. People go to counseling for many reasons, like family problems, problems at school, feeling lonely, relationship difficulties, or just coping with the pressures of being a teenager.

Counselors are men and women who have been trained to listen to your concerns and problems and help you find some answers. Counselors can be psychologists, psychiatrists, social workers, guidance counselors, and other trained individuals like nurses and doctors. Counseling is a process to learn about yourself, and it takes time and commitment. There are many types of counselors and treatments. You may need to shop around to find the person that best meshes with your personality.

Counselors try to get you to help yourself go from one stage to another, to lead a life without pain and sadness as the main focus. Private counseling usually takes place once or twice a week for one-hour sessions. You can discuss your emotions and try to come to some answers. If the therapist is a psychiatrist or a doctor who can prescribe medications, drug therapy may be offered, especially if he or she sees that you are feeling very depressed and very anxious. Doctors may recommend antidepressants to treat your depression.

Antidepressant medication is used to correct a chemical imbalance or chemical disruption in a person's brain. A doctor has to write a prescription for the medication. There are many on the market, and the doctor may have you go through a series of trial medications before you find the one that is most appropriate for you. If you have an addiction to alcohol and/or drugs, a treatment facility may be offered as well.

A counselor may assess your risk of being suicidal. When you talk to a counselor, they will try to familiarize themselves with your sources of stress and your coping mechanisms. A counselor will look for any suicidal warning signs that you may be exhibiting, and if he or she determines that you are at risk, the counselor can then offer interventions to support you. All suicide signs are taken very seriously. If you have a suicide plan, be open and share it with your counselor. Also, your counselor needs to know if you have attempted suicide before. With your counselor's support, you will learn to manage your stress. Your counselor will help monitor you so that you have somewhere to go if you are starting to feel that you are spiraling out of control.

TYPES OF COUNSELING

Cognitive Behavioral Therapy

Many suicidal teens have these three negative views:

1. a Negative view of themselves

2. a Negative view of the world

3. a Negative view of the future or a sense of hopelessNess

A cognitive behavioral therapist focuses on your cognition, or how you see your own reality and interpret your world. The therapist helps you get insight into how you are seeing the world. The sessions usually last about twelve weeks, approximately twenty sessions or more. With this therapy, there also needs to be time to build a relationship with the therapist.

Family Therapy

Family counseling is meeting with a counselor and your family to talk about the individual and group dynamics in your family. This is a way to hear what each member in the family is saying and try to create family dynamics that will work for you in a more positive manner. Some of the goals of family therapy are:

- Get you to see your place in the family

- Get you to see the family dynamics and make good changes

- Get your parents to understand the seriousness of the suicidal threat or attempt

- Get the whole family to work together in an appropriate and supportive manner to help you

- Get your family to understand their conflicts and how to solve them among themselves

Family therapy can be important in helping teens, but each member of the family must be willing to participate and work together to make the changes that are needed. Family therapists are trained in understanding family dynamics and can help your family work together.

Group Therapy

Group counseling is when you meet in a small group with others who have similar problems as you. It is a way to hear others who may share some of your own feelings. It also allows you an opportunity to offer your own perspective with peers your own age or people who have undergone similar traumas. Group therapy works well with many teens, as it reaffirms their feelings that they are not the only ones who have these inner thoughts. In order for group therapy to be successful, it has to be run by good leaders

Group therapy is a great way to work through problems with people who understand what you're feeling.

who can help support the dynamics between the individuals and the full group.

TAKING ANTIDEPRESSANTS

When a doctor feels that you have a tendency toward depression, medication may be prescribed. Unfortunately, there is no "antisuicide" pill that can be prescribed to make someone all better. There are antidepressant medications to stabilize your mood and relieve your symptoms, and there are other medications to control accompanying anxiety and excessive eating and sleeping. It appears that medication alone is not the sole answer in supporting people who experience suicidal thoughts. You will probably need a combination of medication and talk therapy.

FINDING A THERAPIST

To get a therapist, you usually need a referral. Your family doctor can give you one. There can be a cost for some therapists. However, some therapists have sliding scales (rates that are adjusted based on a patient's family income), and some are connected to agencies that may help you in your time of crisis. Your parents might also have a drug or health plan that will cover the cost of your treatment. Again, sometimes you may need to shop around to get a therapist you can connect with.

OVERCOMING SUICIDAL THOUGHTS

Many teens who experience suicidal thoughts say that they feel hopeless. They don't believe their lives will ever feel different, and they don't think there are solutions to their depression. Remember that feelings are not facts. There are countless resources for teens who are suicidal. Friends, family, and teachers want to help you feel better and see you live a life free of suicidal thoughts. Help is out there. The first step is reaching out.

Dialectical Behavior Therapy (DBT)

Researchers are constantly studying new therapies, medications, and treatments for mental health conditions of all kinds. One reason to stay positive about the future is the progress that scientists and medical professionals are making in treating depression and suicidal thoughts. In the past, experts have noted that it is difficult to treat teens. However, in 2018, a therapy called dialectical behavior therapy (DBT) became the first treatment backed by research for helping teens fight suicidal thoughts and behaviors.

DBT was developed by Dr. Marsha M. Linehan. It is a variation of cognitive behavioral therapy that involves weekly sessions with a therapist and weekly group therapy sessions. DBT is known for giving people the tools to deal with situations that may cause big, emotional responses.

Dr. Linehan created DBT in the late 1980s. She shared her own story of grappling with mental illness for the first time in 2011. Dr. Linehan suffered with a condition called borderline personality disorder in her teens and was hospitalized for treatment at the age of seventeen. Over time, she overcame the urge to harm herself.

Dr. Linehan says that so-called radical acceptance was what changed everything. Radical acceptance became a core part of DBT. The *New York Times* describes it this way, "two seemingly opposed principles [form] the basis of [DBT]: acceptance of life as it is, not as it is supposed to be; and the need to change, despite that reality and because of it." In other words, there is power in accepting yourself and your life exactly as it is now. Yet you can accept yourself and your life while still working to make it better, happier, and more fulfilling.

Chapter 4

Hope and Healing

Not all the news about teen suicide trends is bad news. Research shows that several kinds of suicide prevention programs reduce the number of student suicide attempts. In particular, programs that teach warning signs and fight the stigma of depression help teens to help themselves and others.

Prevention can be seen as circular, involving three connected stages. Primary prevention aims to reduce

Opposite: Suicide prevention programs at schools are making a big difference in the number of student suicide attempts.

the risk of suicide by concentrating on improving the physical, emotional, and spiritual well-being of at-risk people. Secondary prevention (early intervention) tries to target suicidal individuals either before they injure themselves or during a suicidal crisis. Tertiary prevention (postvention) focuses on individuals who have been affected by suicidal behavior: ones who

Students at Logansport High School in Indiana are helping their classmates by participating in the Sources of Strength suicide prevention program.

have attempted it, those who are at high risk for recurrence, and family members who are also at high risk.

PRIMARY PREVENTION

Prevention is education. Prevention programs include lessons on life skills and parenting, crisis hotlines, and support for high-risk families, and there are trained professionals to do screenings, assessments, and prevention work. Suicide prevention education includes parental education. Teaching parents to learn about suicide's warning signs, the significance of developing their child's and their own self-esteem, developing trust with their child, and the need for parenting courses, especially on how to parent an adolescent, are all part of the education.

Peer education in schools could include topics like the warning signs of depression and suicide, how to deal with stress appropriately, and sexuality. Community education could also include warning signs like copycat suicides, developing community resources for teens, initiating suicide prevention programs, offering grief support groups, and generally developing positive attitudes toward teens so they will seek help in their own communities.

Teen self-education needs to include what leads up to suicide, how to cope, whom to talk to when they require help, and having access to school curriculum dealing with suicide.

There is strong evidence indicating the treatment of alcohol and drug abuse can reduce suicide rates. Lessons about the hazards of substance abuse

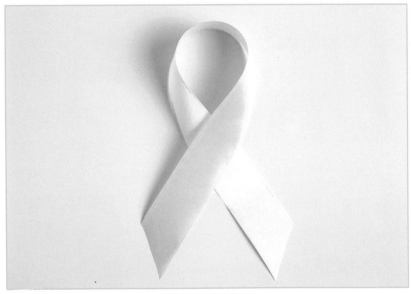

Yellow ribbons represent suicide prevention efforts.

should also be addressed at school. Some effective interventions involve gun control. In a household in which a firearm is kept, it is three times more likely that an inhabitant will die from suicide than a person who is living in a gun-free home.

Suicide Intervention Programs in Schools

Many schools have suicide awareness and intervention programs. The program may start by addressing what suicide is. You and your classmates may know or not know about key information about suicide, including common myths.

You might also learn about how you can tell if someone is suicidal. This might be done by identifying what is normal adolescent emotional development, like mood swings, from suicidal warning signs. Doing a role-playing exercise with a friend in which one person says how he or she is experiencing depression while the other friend reacts appropriately is also a good exercise.

There may be a discussion on why teens attempt suicide. Some of the discussion might focus on stress. For example, you might find a partner and both list all the stresses in your lives. Hook up with another group of two people and see if you match or can add more. At the end of the activity, you can list all the causes of stress and then talk about what you can all do to relieve stress.

These sessions might include a lesson about active listening. It is important to talk about how you can help someone who is feeling suicidal. First, always try to be a good listener. Here are questions to ask yourself in evaluating your listening skills:

- Name a time when you were a good listener.

- Name a time when you were a poor listener.

- When did you pay attention?

- When were you too busy to pay attention?

- Did you make good eye contact?

- Were you distracted when somebody was trying to talk to you?

- Were you empathetic to somebody else's feelings?

- Were you interested in what somebody else had to say?

Suicide intervention programs might also involve discussions about alcohol and drug abuse. A young adult who is recovering from substance abuse could come to your school to talk about his or her experiences.

If your school is not sensitized to or aware of the problem of suicide, here are some ideas to get started in the community:

- See if your school can start a peer counseling program.

- Make sure your school has guidelines in place for suicides, bullying, cyberbullying, high-risk behaviors, and depression.

- Find out what is already available in your community.

- Ask your local law enforcement agency about guidelines for restricting access to firearms for young people.

- Contact your local crisis line and ask what it has available in resources for education and training.

- Ask your local emergency services (paramedics, ambulances) about procedures and follow-up for people who attempt suicide.

- Create a website to inform individuals about services and resources.

- Help organize suicide awareness or intervention skills training.

- Get involved with staff at your school to create a suicide prevention plan.

EARLY INTERVENTION

Intervention is the care and treatment of the person who is in crisis or who has suicidal concerns. It involves evaluating and managing a crisis situation.

In school suicide-intervention programs, the school develops systems to provide immediate help to high-risk students and establishes policies and procedures as well as links to outside community resources that do follow-up with students. Counseling in the school focuses on the severity of the student risk and immediately prevents self-harm and stabilizes the student's current level of coping. There is a

School guidance counselors are an important part of early intervention programs.

reduction in suicide rates of young people when there have been school-based interventions, such as crisis management, self-esteem enhancement, development of coping skills, and assistance in helping to make healthy decisions.

There are many ways to do interventions. Some of these treatments might start with a survey that determines a person's suicide risk level. A person may also start psychotherapy, which is a term used for different kinds of psychological counseling. Some methods include teaching people how to think positively and to develop coping and problem-solving skills. In therapy, a person may also undergo interpersonal therapy, which may include teaching social skills, such as making friends.

Psychotherapy doesn't have to be one-on-one. A person can join group therapy, meaning meeting people of the same age or with the same depressive illnesses. Family therapy is when everybody in your family participates in therapy sessions, either one-on-one or together as a family. There are also various supports at school, such as the school nurse, guidance counselors, psychologists, and social workers.

A person who is depressed can also use relaxation and visualization therapies, and biofeedback, which aims to correct stress level. Antidepressant medications are another way to fight depression.

If the depression is severe enough, a person might require hospitalization. Once a suicide has been attempted, hospitalization may also be necessary. This may entail confinement in the psychiatric ward of a hospital and placing the patient on suicide watch and all staff on high alert. Although hospitalization may seem scary, it is a time in which specialists can help direct the next steps in preventing reoccurrence, like assessing for drug and alcohol abuse. This is also a time that you may be treated with medications like antidepressants or antianxiety drugs as well as making sure you have somebody to go to for counseling when you leave the hospital.

In the time following a suicide, it's critical to support friends and classmates.

POSTVENTION

The days and weeks after a suicide can be filled with confusion and turmoil. Postvention refers to the steps schools should take in the aftermath of a suicide to help the students, staff, and parents. After a student has died by suicide, coordinated services and activities designed to help students, parents, friends, teachers, and the community cope are necessary.

The death of a student by suicide is very difficult for staff and students at the deceased's school. Some of the major concerns that need to be addressed are grief resolution and making sure that a suicide death does not inspire copycat suicides in a school community. Professionals can help support the family and friends who have been profoundly affected by the suicide of their loved one through individual and group counseling and support.

High-risk students should be sought out to be counseled and monitored. The funeral and memorial services should be handled with grace and dignity. It should be recognized that any student who dies by suicide was part of the community and will be missed as his or her life had meaning and value.

Here's what you can expect a counselor to do after the suicide of a peer:

- Help you accept the reality of the loss. It is important to give yourself permission to grieve in your own way, as long as it is not detrimental to yourself or others.

- Help you to identify and express your feelings. You may have feelings of regret, anger, and guilt. Both positive and negative feelings may need to be expressed in a safe and empathetic environment.

- You may learn about typical grief reactions in an effort to normalize your experience. In the grieving process, there will be highs and lows, much like being on an emotional roller coaster.

- You may experience feelings of lack of control, which is not unusual.

- You may be cautioned against not allowing yourself to grieve or hurrying your grief process.

Remember that grief is individualistic, there is no right or wrong way to grieve. It may take you a long time to feel happy or even laugh again.

SURVIVORS OF SUICIDE

Once a teen has died by suicide, many people are affected. The devastated family and friends are known as "survivors." There are millions of survivors each year trying to deal with the loss of their loved ones who died by suicide. Suicide-loss survivors suffer in three ways: first, because they are grieving for the deceased; second, because they are suffering from the traumatic experience; and third, because people do not talk about suicide. It can be difficult to confide in your closest friends and family members. You might not receive the response you may have received if it was another kind of death.

After a loved one has taken their life, you may go through a series of emotional ups and downs. You might experience initial shock. You might feel it is all a bad dream and when you wake up things will be back to normal. You might have bouts of crying and feel blue or tired. Your sleeping patterns may suffer as well. After a suicide, survivors within the family often experience feelings of guilt and often want to punish themselves for what has happened. You may torture yourself with thoughts about whether you could have done something different. If so, would the person be alive today? You may constantly ask or say to yourself:

- What if ... ?

- Why didn't I ... ?

- If only I could have ...

- Suicide cheated me out of time to say goodbye.

- I had no chance to say, "I'm sorry."

- I'm feeling helpless.

- I feel vulnerable. I'm afraid it will happen to others in my family.

- Why didn't I see the warning signs?

- Why?

Many times in your head you will go over and over the last conversation or the last time you saw your loved one alive. You may start experiencing nightmares.

WORKING THROUGH GRIEF

Each person grieves differently and at his or her own pace. Remember, you may not be at the same stage as your other family members or friends. There is no correct timing for grieving. Some people may stay longer in certain stages than others. The stages of grief are:

- Denial (This isn't happening to me!)

- Anger (why is this happening to me?)

- Bargaining (I promise I'll be a better person if ...)

- Depression (I don't care anymore.)

- Acceptance (I'm ready for whatever comes.)

It is important that you do not hold back your emotions. Let them out. Cry. Talk to your friends. You may need to take the initiative to talk about the suicide or share your feelings. Many people do not know what to say after a person dies by suicide. It might be up to you to open the channels of

Coping with a Parent's Suicide

Creating traditions for special days like Mother's Day or Father's Day can help you cope with the loss of a parent.

Losing a parent is one of the most traumatic experiences a teen can go through. Losing a parent to suicide can often cause a confusing mixture of emotions. It is normal to experience feelings of anger, numbness, shame, or even relief if a parent was struggling for a long time prior to taking their own life. Experts say that it is critical to allow yourself to feel these feelings and work through them as part of the grieving process.

Keep in mind that some days will be easier than others. Difficult days might include Mother's Day, Father's Day, your parent's birthday, and the anniversary of their death. Mental health professionals advise preparing for days that may prove difficult.

Psychologists recommend creating new traditions for these days, traditions that celebrate the life of the person you lost. That said, always check in with yourself. If you need time alone on those days, let the people around you know. If you need extra support, communicate that too.

Facing questions about your parent's death is also something to prepare for. Plan out what you'll say in advance of questions so that you're not taken off guard. It's OK to tell people that you don't want to talk about your parent's death. The American Society for Suicide Prevention suggests the following responses to questions or comments that violate your boundaries:

- **I don't really want to talk about it right now.**
- **That comment is very hurtful to me; you know my [parent] just died.**
- **It really is none of your business.**

Grief is hard work, but you don't have to go through it alone. Reach out to friends and family. Join a support group for teens who have lost a parent to suicide. And if you begin to have suicidal thoughts yourself, ask for help immediately.

communication. You may find it helpful to reach out to family and friends. Many times, clergy is around the family to provide comfort. This could be a time to look to your religion for some comfort.

Your Feelings Are Normal

Suicide is usually a culmination of a sequence of disturbing and troubling events. Depending on the relationship you had with the deceased, you may have been already living in a nightmare without control, and now that it is over there is a feeling of relief. You may feel ashamed for having these feelings.

There may also be a feeling of guilt, which might come from the relief that you feel that the person who died by suicide finally did it, guilty at not being able to stop the act, or guilty for blaming God. You may review the past because you may feel you have failed the person, and you want to try and discover how.

Many survivors also feel shame because the act of suicide is not condoned by their religion, town, family, or in general, society. You also may start blaming either yourself or others.

Dwelling on the suicide and picturing it in your head over and over is not beneficial. You may try to remember the kind and good acts of the deceased. The expectation that you will eventually find the "why" for the suicide is one of the first things you may have to let go of on the way to healing. You cannot turn back the clock or erase the past. It is important to find someone or a group that you can relate to that will be a positive influence in your life and help you get to the stage of acceptance and support you through your grieving process.

Grieving for a Sibling

If you have a sibling who died by suicide, you are a very vulnerable survivor. You must struggle with your own grief, as well as guilt, anger, sadness, and all other strong emotions. Unfortunately, your parents are also dealing with their own grief at the same time. They might want to give you the attention that you need but may not feel they have the strength to do it. You may start feeling neglected and troubled, or you might take on a parental role and view your parents as the children.

You need to be able to heal together as a family. Blaming each other will not help. Talking together and sharing emotions will be better for everyone in the long run. If you have young siblings in your family, they may not understand the reactions around them. They may feel the death is their fault, or they may feel abandoned by their loved one. They may benefit from child-oriented therapy, like play or art therapy.

Healing After a Loved One's Suicide

If you have been affected by someone close to you who has taken their own life, bereavement groups are excellent for support. Information on finding one close to you can be found on the internet. Some are affiliated with local hospitals or medical centers. Often members of these groups talk about their own experiences and how they've learned to live with their loss.

Eventually, you will laugh and enjoy your life again. You may have mixed emotions for feeling this way, but remember your feelings are natural and normal. To start the healing process, it is really important that you take care of your own personal well-being. You should eat right, exercise, and try

Finding someone to talk to about your loss is important for healing.

to get enough sleep. This is not the time to take up risky behaviors like smoking, drinking, drugs, and sex just to drown out or not deal with your feelings.

You may need to go to a bereavement group or see a social worker, psychologist, psychiatrist, school guidance counselor, clergy person, or any professional person whom you feel comfortable enough to talk to and whom you feel can guide you through the therapeutic experience. There are also crisis intervention hotlines and centers that are staffed by trained personnel who offer guidance and support while you grieve.

MAKING A DIFFERENCE

If you are experiencing suicidal thoughts, you are not alone. Likewise, if you have lost someone you care about to suicide, you are not alone. The people around you care about you and want you to stay safe, just like you want to protect your friends from harm. Even if it feels like no one cares, there are places to turn where you'll be heard, respected, and helped.

Katie Stubblefield's Second Chance

In 2017, Katie Stubblefield became the youngest American ever to receive a face transplant. A suicide attempt in 2014 required her to have more than twenty facial reconstructive surgeries before the transplant took place. The transplant surgery was performed by eleven surgeons over the course of nearly fifty hours total.

Stubblefield's experience serves as a reminder that not everyone who attempts suicide suffers from depression. At eighteen, she made her attempt in the heat of the moment, after a bad breakup and medical and family issues.

She has shared her story in the hopes of preventing others from taking their lives. In spite of years of medical treatment and a difficult recovery, Stubblefield sees only the joy in life. She is grateful to have a second chance. She says, "Life is precious, and life is beautiful. Life is a gift." Stubblefield hopes to spread her message to as many people as possible. She aims to work as a counselor and motivational speaker after she finishes college. Luckily, she has her whole life ahead of her to spread her message of hope and healing.

Call a crisis line. Ask a friend, teacher, or parent if you can take a minute to talk. Remember that some problems might seem big now that won't affect your adult life at all. Other problems, like grief over losing someone you love, won't always feel overwhelming to you. Instead, you'll work through your grief and honor your loved one's memory by building a healthy, happy life. You can use your pain to help others experiencing the same obstacles as you have. Ask for help. Help someone around you. The world will be better for it.

Glossary

anorexia nervosa A serious eating disorder in which a person restricts his or her food intake.

assessment An evaluation, usually performed by a doctor, of a person's mental, emotional, and social capabilities.

assimilation The process by which a minority group gradually adapts to the customs of the larger culture.

bipolar A mental disorder that involves episodes of mania and depression.

chronic Lasting a long period of time.

clinical depression A state of depression so severe as to require treatment.

cluster suicides Two or more suicides that happen around the same time or in the same way; also called copycat suicides.

depression The condition of feeling sad and hopeless.

disempower To take away someone's control of a situation.

hotline A call center in which professionals trained to help with a problem answer phone lines.

pessimism A tendency to dwell on the negative.

prevalent Commonly occurring.

psychiatry The branch of medicine that deals with the diagnosis, treatment, and prevention of mental and emotional disorders.

stigma An unfair feeling of disapproval that causes shame.

suicide The act of intentionally taking one's own life.

suicide rate The percentage of people in a specific group who take their own lives in a certain duration of time.

warning signs Specific observable behaviors, actions, and circumstances of an individual in crisis. These symptoms may indicate that the individual is at risk of suicide.

Further Information

BOOKS

Cartlidge, Cherese. *Teens and Suicide*. Teen Mental Health. San Diego, CA: ReferencePoint Press, 2017.

Landau, Jennifer. *Teens Talk about Suicide, Death, and Grieving*. Teen Voices: Real Teens Discuss Real Problems. New York: Rosen Publishing, 2018.

Toner, Jacqueline B., and Claire A. B. Freeland. *Depression: A Teen's Guide to Survive and Thrive*. Washington, DC: Magination Press, 2016.

WEBSITES
#BeThe1To
http://www.bethe1to.com/resources
Explore tip sheets that cover topics ranging from warning signs to what to do in a crisis on this site hosted by the National Alliance for Suicide Prevention and the National Suicide Prevention Lifeline.

The Jason Foundation: Students
http://www.jasonfoundation.com/get-involved/student
The Jason Foundation provides students with links to teen suicide statistics, materials for student prevention

programs, and an app designed to help you help your friends.

SAVE: Suicide Awareness Voices of Education

http://www.save.org

Take a depression screening, access resources for suicide survivors, and more.

The Trevor Project

https://www.thetrevorproject.org

Find a wealth of suicide prevention resources for LGBTQ youth, including instant messaging with a crisis counselor.

VIDEOS

Kevin Breel: Confessions of a Depressed Comic

https://www.ted.com/talks/kevin_breel_confessions_of_a_depressed_comic

Watch Breel's viral TED Talk about overcoming suicidal thoughts.

Teen Suicide Prevention

https://www.youtube.com/watch?v=3BByqa7bhto

This video by the Mayo Clinic discusses warning signs and what to say to a suicidal teen.

Bibliography

American Foundation for Suicide Prevention. "Suicide Statistics." Retrieved October 1, 2018. https://afsp.org/about-suicide/suicide-statistics.

Beaton, Susan, Peter Forster, and Myfanwy Maple. "Suicide and Language: Why We Shouldn't Use the 'C' Word." *InPsych 2013*, February 2013. https://www.psychology.org.au/publications/inpsych/2013/february/beaton.

Borchard, Therese J. "Marsha Linehan: What Is Dialectical Behavioral Therapy (DBT)?" PsychCentral, June 28, 2011. https://psychcentral.com/blog/marsha-linehan-what-is-dialectical-behavioral-therapy-dbt.

Carey, Benedict. "Expert on Mental Illness Reveals Her Own Struggle." *New York Times*, June 23, 2011. https://www.nytimes.com/2011/06/23/health/23lives.html.

Centers for Disease Control and Prevention. "Suicide among Youth." Retrieved October 1, 2018. https://www.cdc.gov/healthcommunication/toolstemplates/entertainmented/tips/SuicideYouth.html.

Gregory, Christina. "Suicide and Suicide Prevention." PsyCom. Retrieved October 1, 2018. http://www.psycom.net/depression.central.suicide.html.

Kaslow, Nadine. "What to Do If You're Worried about Suicide." Child Mind Institute. Retrieved October 1, 2018. https://childmind.org/article/youre-worried-suicide.

National Institute of Mental Health. "Therapy Reduces Risk in Suicidal Youth." June 27, 2018. https://www.nimh.nih.gov/news/science-news/2018/therapy-reduces-risk-in-suicidal-youth.shtml.

National Suicide Prevention Lifeline. "Professional Initiatives." Retrieved October 1, 2018. https://suicidepreventionlifeline.org/professional-initiatives.

O'Donnell, Jayne, and Anne Saker. "Teen Suicide Is Soaring. Do Spotty Mental Health and Addiction Treatment Share the Blame?" *USA Today*, March 19, 2018. https://www.usatoday.com/story/news/politics/2018/03/19/teen-suicide-soaring-do-spotty-mental-health-and-addiction-treatment-share-blame/428148002.

Phillips, Kristine. "Her Texts Pushed Him to Suicide, Prosecutors Say. But Does That Mean She Killed Him?" *Washington Post*, June 6, 2017. https://www.washingtonpost.com/news/morning-mix/wp/2017/06/06/just-do-it-babe-woman-accused-of-pushing-her-boyfriend-to-kill-himself-is-on-trial-this-week/?utm_term=.2babcb8ed21c.

Provincial Injury Prevention Program, Alberta Health Services. "Suicide: The Language of Suicide." June 14, 2018. https://myhealth.alberta.ca/Alberta/Pages/the-language-of-suicide.aspx.

Rudlin, Kathryn. "What to Say to a Suicidal Teen." Verywell Mind, August 16, 2017. https://www.verywellmind.com/what-to-say-to-a-suicidal-teen-2611331.

SAVE. "Suicide Statistics." Retrieved October 1, 2018. https://save.org/about-suicide/suicide-facts.

Serani, Deborah. "Understanding Survivors of Suicide Loss." *Psychology Today*, November 25, 2013. https://www.psychologytoday.com/us/blog/two-takes-depression/201311/understanding-survivors-suicide-loss.

World Health Organization. "Mental Health: Community Engagement Toolkit." Retrieved October 1, 2018. https://www.who.int/mental_health/suicide-prevention/en.

Index

Index

grief, stages of, 93
group therapy, 71–72, **71**, 74, 86, 98

high-risk behavior, 32–33, 83, 100
Hispanics, 41, 44–46
hotline, 57, 62, 64–65, 79, 100

Indigenous Canadians, 41, 43
intervention, 24, 61–62, 68, 78, 81, 83–86, 100

myths about suicide, 19, 22–27, 81

National Minority Mental Health Awareness Month, **45**, 46
National Suicide Prevention Lifeline, 7, 49, 65
Native Americans, 41–44

pessimism, 14
postvention, 78, 88–90
prevalent, 15, 23, 39
psychiatry, 11, 66–67, 87, 100
psychotherapy, 86

risk factors, 30–31, 43
Roy, Conrad, III, 18–19

seasonal affective disorder (SAD), 15
self-harm or self-destructive behaviors, 16–17, 59, 85
self-medication, 33
stigma, 23, **28**, 34–35, 46, 77
stressors, 9, **38**
Stubblefield, Katie, 101
substance abuse, 8, 80, 83
suicidal ideation, 51
suicidal thoughts, 6–7, 9, 11, 14, 23, 25, 29, 32–33, 41, 44–45, 48, 51–52, 58, 60–63, 72–74, 95, 100
suicide rate, 9, 36, 42, 44, 80, 86
survivors, 11, 91, 96–97

Trevor Project, **46**, 47

warning signs, 12–13, 17, 39, 52, **53**, 68, 77, 79, 81, 92

About the Author

Caitlyn Miller is a writer, editor, and educator whose work often focuses on teens overcoming difficult situations. Miller is the author of eight books for middle- and high-school students. In her free time, she likes to read and travel with her husband.